FIFE EDUCATION
COMMITTEE

KING'S ROAD P. SCHOOL
ROSYTH

KT-584-242

Push and Pull

written by Maria Gordon
and
illustrated by Mike Gordon

Wayland

Simple Science

Series Editor: Catherine Baxter
Advice given by Audrey Randall – member of the Science Working Group
for the National Curriculum.

First published in 1995 by
Wayland (Publishers) Ltd
61 Western Road, Hove
East Sussex, BN3 1JD, England

© Copyright 1995 Wayland (Publishers) Ltd

British Library Cataloguing in Publication Data
Gordon, Maria
    Push and Pull. – (Simple Science Series)
    I. Title II. Gordon, Mike III. Series
    531

ISBN 0-7502-1294-2

Typeset by MacGuru
Printed and bound in Italy by G Canale and C.S.p.A., Turin, Italy

Contents

There are two ways to move things. You can push or pull them.

A push moves something away. Use your finger to move a toy car away from you. This is a push.

A pull moves something
nearer. Grip the car with
your finger and thumb.
Move it towards you.
This is a pull.

5

There are many different ways to push and pull.

Some pushing and pulling just happens...

like wind blowing...

plants growing...

and water flowing.

But people and animals can push or pull to help do things...like gather food and build homes.

The things people make which push and pull are called machines. Some machines are very simple like...

knives to push into things...

belts to pull things tight...

brooms to push things away.

Other machines are not so simple like...

the ones pulling hands round a clock...

motors pushing propellers round...

engines pushing rockets into space.

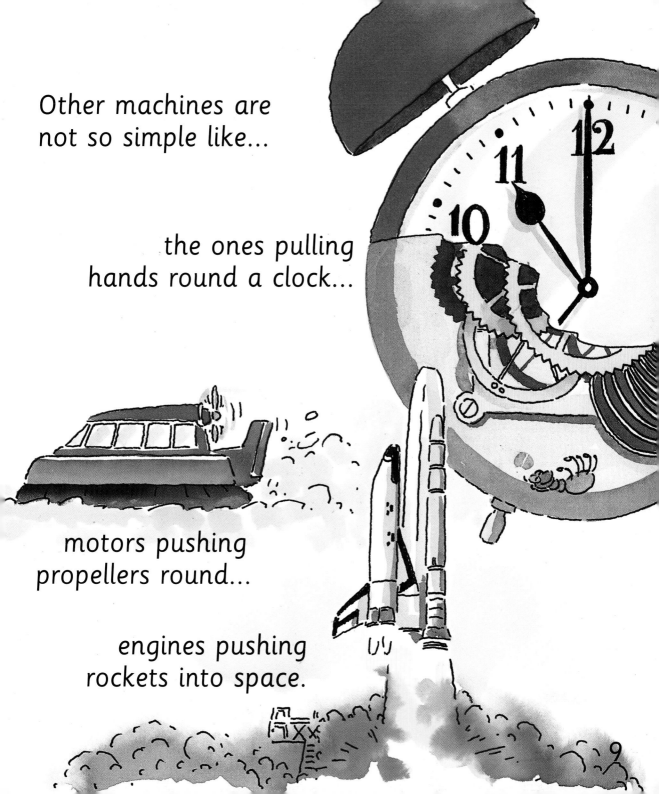

Long ago, cave people rubbed stones together to make fire. They hunted with spears. Later, people also fired stones and arrows. Rubbing, throwing and firing are all kinds of pushing and pulling.

People invented many things to push and pull... like paddles to push through water, wheelbarrows to push heavy things and snow sleds pulled by dogs.

11

Many years ago a scientist called Isaac
Newton watched an apple fall from a tree.
He saw that there was something pulling the
apple to the ground. He called it gravity.

You can see this for yourself. Hold out a ball
and let go. Gravity pulls it to the ground.

If gravity didn't pull people and things down, they would float like astronauts in space!

Isaac Newton showed people important things about pushing and pulling. You can see them too...

Put a toy car on a table. It stays still if it is not pushed or pulled.

A moving toy car keeps going in a straight line unless it is pushed or pulled by something.

A toy car moves when it is pushed or pulled.

Now try pushing or pulling one when it is moving. It will turn, slow down or speed up.

Push a toy car over the edge of a table. Gravity pulls on it. This makes the car turn and fall.

When something is pushed or pulled it pushes or pulls back! Heavy things push or pull back more than light ones. This is why they are harder to move.

Tie an empty plastic pot to a piece of string. Tie the other end to an empty toy truck in the middle of a table. Put plasticine in the pot until it begins to pull the truck.

Fill the truck with plasticine. Now the truck pulls harder. Put more plasticine in the pot to make it pull even more and move the truck.

Pushing and pulling can change the shape
of things. Use your fingers to push and
pull some plasticine or dough and
change its shape.

Make different shapes with your fingers.
Muscles in your arm are pulling your finger bones.
Use your muscles to pull other bones. What shapes can your body make?

When things are pushed or pulled they rub against anything next to them. This is called friction.

Push a toy car on a smooth, flat floor. It cannot keep going for long because it rubs against the floor and even the air.

AIR

Rough things make more friction. Push the toy car on a carpet. It does not go far.

In a real car, brakes rub against the wheels. This friction helps the car to stop.
Smooth ice makes less friction and makes cars hard to stop.

Things that roll make less friction. They need smaller pushes and pulls to make them move.

Push a coin on its edge. Now push a coin lying flat. The first coin rolls. It needs less push.

Heavy things need bigger pushes and pulls to make them move. Push a football. It rolls, but it needs more push than a coin on its edge. Why?

Look at cars and lorries.
You can see the big ones need bigger
engines to pull their wheels round and
start them moving.

23

How much pushing and pulling do you do?

Feel your feet push against the ground when you run or walk.

Push the pedals on a bike.

With a grown-up, pull the oars on a boat.
Watch the oars push against the water.

Pull the peel from an orange.

Push a toy car down a slope...
Push against it to make it stop.

Pushing and pulling changes things
around you.

Wind pushes trees and
changes their shape...
The sea pushes so long
and hard it makes holes
in rocks...Gravity changes
the shape of the land
when it pulls down
rocks.

People and machines pull up plants from the land... Diggers push earth around...and look out! Moving bikes, cars and lorries can push into things and change their shape...even yours!

How many different ways can you see pushing and pulling being used here? Where is friction being made?

Which things here need a big push or pull?
See how hard you can push and pull.

Notes for adults

The 'Simple Science' series helps children to reach Key Stage 1:
Attainment Targets 1-4 of the Science National Curriculum.
Below are some suggestions to help complement and extend the
learning in this book.

4/5   Look for the push or pull behind the movements in simple,
ordinary tasks such as turning the pages of this book.

6/7   Spot plants and tree roots pushing up through soil and man-
made surfaces. Make a display showing how animals push
and pull, e.g. elephant's trunk, bird's beak, cat's paw. Read
Rudyard Kipling's 'Just So' story, *'The Elephant's Child'*.

8/9   Look inside a clockwork mechanism. Compare the workings of
moving toys. Make levers with rulers. Use simple tools. Show
how one movement is used to make another one. Go on a
supervised tour around a factory.

10/11   Make a history chart showing different inventions around the
world from prehistoric skin scrapers to bicycles: how do they
incorporate pushing or pulling?

12/13   Demonstrate magnetism as another natural force. Show
repulsion and attraction of poles.

14/15   Use toy cars to show connection between the strength of a
push or pull and speed. See how parts of musical instruments
are pushed or pulled and make quiet or loud sounds.

16/17   Look at animals in harness. What loads do they pull?
Compare transport in different countries.

18/19   Do P.E. Discuss how bodies use energy from food and change
it into energy to make muscles pull. Show how muscles

always pull even when they help to push.

20/21 Sit and slide on polished floors and carpeted ones. Oil bicycles, soap some screws. Go ice-skating. Look at racing tyres, skis, ice-hockey pucks etc. Make an aerodynamics display with vehicle photos, paper darts, seeds etc.

22/23 Research the history of the wheel, construction of the pyramids etc. Set a load moving problem with boxes, blocks, string and cardboard rolls.

24/25 Make a push and pull montage. Read about the 'Pushmi-pullyu' in Hugh Lofting's *'The Story of Dr. Doolittle'*.

26/27 Take a road safety walk: look out for screeching brakes, skid marks, dented cars etc. Point out behaviour which avoids these!

28/29 Do some furniture re-arranging. Estimate the amount of pushing and pulling involved. Hold a tug-of-war!

Other books to read

Forces by G. Peacock (Wayland, 1994)
Gravity by Janice Vancleave (Wiley, 1993)
Pushing and Pulling by K.Davies and W. Oldfield (Wayland, 1992)
Starting and Stopping by B. Knapp (Atlantic, 1992)

Index